IMAGES
of America

SUDBURY

Along the Sudbury River in 1906, mounds of hay, known as haycocks, are seen in the distance. The mounds were gathered by farmers on wood stakes to dry. The hay was what attracted the original settlers and led to the publication of William Wood's *New England Prospect* in 1633, which states, "These marshes be rich ground and bring plenty of hay." Farmers sought this rich reed grass and reed canary grass (now almost extinct) to fatten their cattle. The gun punt boat in the foreground was used for hunting. (Photograph by Hattie Goodnow.)

ON THE COVER: Dominion Day in Sudbury, Massachusetts, was the idea of George J. Raymond, the owner of Raymond's Department Stores. On every July 1 from 1905 until 1915, Raymond brought all of his 1,000 employees on a train to South Sudbury, where they walked a mile through his extensive estate dressed in whites and reds with brass bands leading them to a grand banquet and games. Raymond became a millionaire with the success of his stores, which were famous for the slogan, "Where you bot the hat?" Raymond, who was Canadian and employed many Canadians, advertised "Quality goods at the lowest possible price for cash." (Courtesy of the Sudbury Historical Society, Inc.)

IMAGES
of America

SUDBURY

Sudbury Historical Society, Inc.

ARCADIA
PUBLISHING

Published by Arcadia Publishing
Charleston, South Carolina

Library of Congress Control Number: 2012937098

For all general information, please contact Arcadia Publishing:
Telephone 843-853-2070
Fax 843-853-0044
E-mail sales@arcadiapublishing.com
For customer service and orders:
Toll-Free 1-888-313-2665

Visit us on the Internet at www.arcadiapublishing.com

This book is dedicated to our late volunteer, Virginia A. "Ginny" Maenpaa, and to Taka Morita, a former intern from Japan and a loyal contributor since 2000.

CONTENTS

ACKNOWLEDGMENTS

The completion of such a large project is generally beyond the scope of one or two people. We would like to thank the people of Sudbury for all of their donations, which have resulted in the collections now preserved at the Sudbury Historical Society, Inc. (SHS). Their pictures, objects, books, and art have helped make up the history of the town.

We would also like to thank the Sudbury Foundation for its financial support, Town Manager Maureen G. Valente, and Town Clerk Rosemary Harvell for permission to use images under their responsibility.

The society would like to thank the book committee members and staff: Mary Collins Vivaldi, SHS president and committee member; Ursula Lyons, SHS vice president, committee member, Arcadia publishing liaison, and editor; Chuck Zimmer, who created a relational database, completed high-quality scanning and picture restoration, and whose skills this book would not have been possible without; Lee Swanson, the curator/archivist for the Sudbury Historical Society, Inc., who provided the inspiration to start this project, was a continuous source of information about people, places, and events, and was recently named town historian; Nancy Somers, a society trustee and committee member who provided unique military pictures; Joan Meenan, a society trustee and committee member whose weekly commitment to the committee chair was invaluable; and Beth Gray-Nix, a society trustee and committee chair who spearheaded and organized the project through its completion.

Unless otherwise noted, all images are courtesy of the Sudbury Historical Society, Inc.

INTRODUCTION

In 1638, Sudbury attracted its first settlers because of its slow moving river, its rich reed grass and reed canary grass used to fatten cattle, and its good land to grow what was needed. On September 4, 1639, the settlement in Sudbury became incorporated, as shelters were built on the east side of the river in what was the original Sudbury but is now Wayland. A primitive wooden bridge was built across the river to the west side, which was also settled, starting in the 1650s. This west settlement is now known as the town of Sudbury.

Sudbury remained an agricultural town but was aided in its connection to larger cities, like Boston, by the arrival of railroad lines and the King's Highway, later called the Boston Post Road, which became a route going west. Weary travelers often stopped for food, drink, and lodging at the inns along the way. The oldest inn is now called Longfellow's Wayside Inn and has been a popular inn and restaurant in almost continuous existence since 1716.

The 19th century did not change Sudbury much, as people still lived simply and frugally. As they had in the Revolutionary War, Sudbury sent its men to serve in the Civil War, World Wars I and II, and the Korean War. Sudbury remained a sheltered community until World War II, when the population began to grow from less than 2,000 to today's 18,000 in six decades.

Flower growing in greenhouses became very popular, and a few large companies, like Raytheon and Sperry Rand, moved into Sudbury. In the last 30 years, Sudbury has improved its schools and town services and built larger, more affluent homes. It continues to have a strong sense of community and a desirable quality of life, which make it one of the most attractive towns west of Boston.

The Sudbury Historical Society, Inc., has sampled its archives to provide fleeting windows through which readers can glimpse the town's history. We know that many important people and places are not included, as we could only choose from what was generously given to us over the years. We chose the chapters in the hope that everyone who has ever had a connection with Sudbury will find something that awakens a warm memory of the town.

One

AGRICULTURE

In 1905, Hattie J. Goodnow won a top prize with her photograph of Goodnow family members haying in their fields on Green Hill in South Sudbury. Haying was a dry, hot job that had to be done on sunny days, as rain would ruin the hay or cause spontaneous combustion in a barn. A stoneware jug of "Haymaker's Switchel" kept in the shade would quench their thirst.

The Willis Place at 333 Maynard Road was built in 1704 by Roger Willis and his son Samuel and stayed in the Willis family until 1881. Its unique features include the present living room, which was the original kitchen, and a walk-in fireplace with a beehive oven. The porch was removed long ago, and the front door was moved to the side of the house. Here, the Willis family poses proudly in front of the house in 1879.

A farmer showed pride of ownership in his property by building a good stone wall or fence to keep the cows in or out or, in this case, to protect his crops. This wall at the Willis Place was removed by the state when it straightened out the road in 1925 and took three parcels by eminent domain. Today, there is a replacement garage where the barn once stood.

Thomas H. Ashe lived as a renter in a private house on King Philip Road in 1916 and did odd jobs in the neighborhood. He was dependable but did take his time, especially if one had not heard a funny story he had just heard. He left his mark in a unique way, signing and dating the back of a cedar clapboard on an outbuilding he had built for a resident of King Philip Road.

Hattie Goodnow, who took the photograph below in 1905 with her wooden box camera, followed the admonition of the magazine *Photo Era*, learning how to compose photographs and to record different themes the magazine suggested like cows, clouds, snow scenes, portraits, haying, and street scenes. She succeeded with a heavy camera, a wooden tripod, and glass-plate negatives. The historical society has more than 250 photographs she produced until the 1930s. She lived at 293 Concord Road.

Bob Walker, the last farmer in Sudbury to plow with a horse, is seen here at his farm at 55–62 Goodman's Hill Road. He had more than 50 acres under cultivation until his death in 1983. The house that once occupied this site was called the Bogle-Walker House. In 1806, Bogle family members built it from white-oak timbers and other wood they brought down from New Hampshire, where they owned land. It had been in the National Register of Historic Places but was torn down on its 200th anniversary.

Bob Walker's truck and barn are seen here. The Walkers' original house was built in 1722 across the street from where the Bogle-Walker House once stood. After Walker died in 1983, the barn was purchased, dismantled, and rebuilt in New Hampshire. Recently, the land has grown houses instead of crops.

These were the dairy buildings at the Bonnie Brook Farm in South Sudbury. In the 1920s, H.P. Hood and Sons bought the farm from Aubrey Borden and made it into a model farm to educate the public about where milk and milk products came from. It is interesting that even in the 1920s, the public was losing touch with the sources of what they ate and drank. Presently, the Raytheon Company is located on this site at 528 Boston Post Road.

This was the cow house, or dairy cow barn, at Bonnie Brook Farm. Hood advertised that their cows lived in a clean, light, airy cow house on the model farm. However, many non-model farms were not well maintained. H.P. Hood and Sons was organized in 1846.

In 1910, the Cavicchio family emigrated from Italy to Sudbury. They started with 56 acres of land, where they developed an orchard and had field-grown vegetables that were delivered and sold in the Boston markets. This portrait was taken about 1923 and shows the Cavicchio family, from left to right, (first row) Virginia; Civita, the mother; James; Giuseppe, the father; and Gaetano "Emmy"; (second row) Paul, Catherine, Anna, and Mary.

Civita and Giuseppe Cavicchio and their two oldest daughters, Anna and Catherine, are working on their farm at 110 Codjer Lane. Over the years, the family has expanded its operation and has become a major grower of quality horticultural products in New England while preserving 200 acres of agricultural land.

Giuseppe Cavicchio shows his pride in his celery in 1925. Beginning in 1928 and continuing until 1938, Henry Ford's agents made continuous offers for the Cavicchio farm, first for all of it and then just 1.5 acres for placement of a dam that would be a part of Ford's Wash Brook Project. The dam would provide waterpower to the Mill Village for an auto parts factory manufacturing Bakelite parts. Cavicchio refused to sell it at the price offered and is often credited with saving Sudbury.

This aerial view shows the Cavicchio farm before the 1938 hurricane that destroyed most of their apple orchard with 120-mile-per-hour winds and gusts up to 186 miles per hour. They were forced to expand into new crops, such as winter squash, zucchini, peppers, greens, carrots, celery, and corn, which were all cultivated and tended by the family and then driven daily to Boston's Quincy Market.

15

This view looks south from Green Hill toward South Sudbury in about 1905. By this time, almost all of the land had been cleared for farming, orchards, and dirt roads all the way to Mount Nobscot. This image shows an almost-idealized landscape of beautifully maintained farms and buildings. But that is the way it was, due to pride in ownership and the importance of good relations with one's

neighbors. King Philip Road is to the left, the Boston Post Road is in the middle, and Concord Road is to the right. The preponderance of windmills looks strange today, but they were labor saving and added a sound to the landscape, which is rarely heard today.

Capt. Israel Haynes had the house above built in 1840 as a wedding gift for his son Leander Haynes and his wife, Mary Gleason. The house, at 113 Haynes Road, was passed down to Clarence Austin (right) and his wife, Angelina Haynes. The younger child is Herman Austin, who died in 1969. The Haynes family is one of the founding families of Sudbury.

Hubbard Brown (1839–1922) was a farmer and a horticulturist. He originated the practice of growing under glass in Sudbury in 1879 and gained some renown for raising greenhouse cucumbers, which he sold in the winter in Boston for the princely sum of 10¢ a piece. His greenhouse was located at 79 Nobscot Road. After he retired, Brown lived at 16 Concord Road and worked as a real estate agent.

This warming pan is from the home of Deacon William Brown at 79 Nobscot Road. It is made out of brass with a turned walnut handle. The top of the pan lifts up, and coals were put inside. Before central heating existed, one would move it between the sheets and the down comforter to warm up the bed before going to sleep. (Photograph by Chuck Zimmer.)

Hubbard Brown's house and the greenhouses he built are seen here in the 1890s. The house was built in 1780 and was originally situated higher up on the hill. Along with his 10¢ cucumbers, Brown grew tomatoes and celery in the winter, which he took to the Boston market until 1907.

The Aubrey Borden farm was located at 68 Old County Road and stretched over toward Goodman's Hill. Here, the family uses a Model T car engine to power a gadget that chopped corn stalks and then carried them up to the top of the silo. The resulting silage, or green fodder, was then used to feed the cows—a great demonstration of Yankee ingenuity. The 1938 hurricane collapsed the barn, killing 50 cows.

A Yarn Counter does exactly what its name implies. The tops of the mallets were one foot apart, and in a full rotation, there was a length of six feet. The internal mechanism hidden from view was able to automatically count the distance. Part of the machine is called the weasel, and it "pops" at 72 feet, which may be where the nursery rhyme "Pop, goes the weasel" originated in the 1850s. (Gift of John Borden; photograph by Chuck Zimmer.)

The Raymond Farm was at 80 Raymond Road. George J. Raymond (1852–1915) was a wealthy businessman who owned Raymond's Department Stores in the Boston area. Home of Uncle Eph and "Where you bot the hat?" fame, it was in existence from 1879 until 1973. The home was built in 1750 by the Hunt family, but Raymond added a water tower, barns, and many outbuildings, including a mausoleum, on the 500 acres. Stained-glass windows from a steamboat were installed in the house.

This flax hetchel dates from 1690. It was used in one of the many steps in the process of preparing flax so that it could be spun into linen. Flax is an annual herb plant whose fibers are separated by pulling handfuls through the tines of different comb-like devices to separate them after breaking or scutching the fiber. (Gift of Loren Hayden; photograph by Chuck Zimmer.)

John Murray and his wife, Mary, were farmers in South Sudbury. As of 1890, they owned a good amount of farmable land, including the land surrounding the Wadsworth Cemetery. They had six cows, one yearling, one horse, a carriage, two houses, and barn and yet could not "make a go of it." By the time this picture was taken in 1914, they were living hand-to-mouth. There was no Social Security at that time, but the town took care of its own.

The Davis Turkey Farm in South Sudbury was located where the Wayside Carriage House Inn is today at 738 Boston Post Road. The farm operated in the 1930s and the 1940s. At that time, there were a lot of turkey farms in the area to provide freshly killed poultry to the locals and to sell it at Quincy Market in Boston.

This aerial view of the Briardale-Frost Farm was taken in the late 1940s. It was a successful dairy farm in its day, operated by the Frost family in the area of 148 Great Road. Sperry Rand later developed this land. The main house still exists, partially surrounded by the Frost Farm complex of elderly housing.

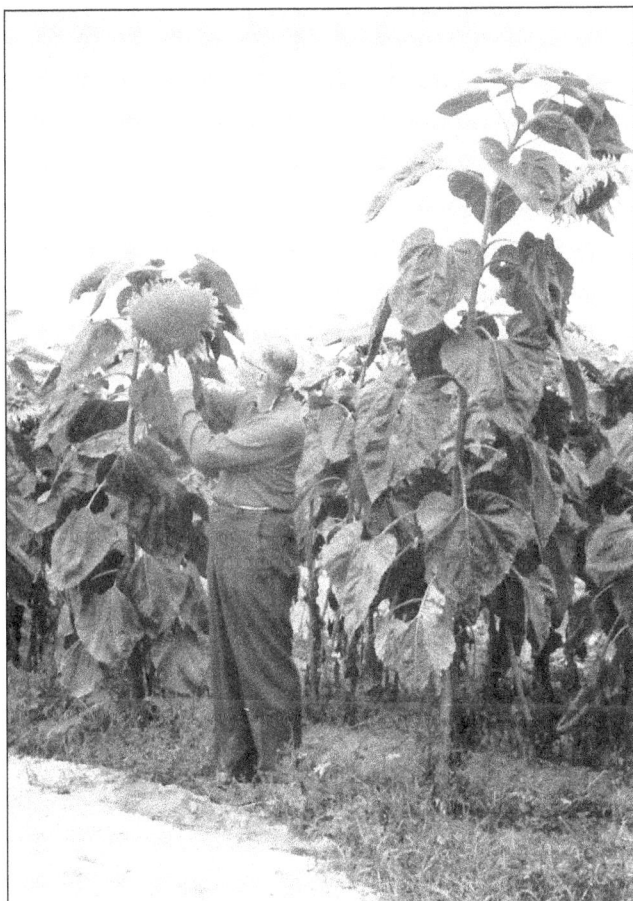

Gurnseyl Frost examines his sunflower crop on Briardale-Frost Farm at 148 Great Road around 1948. Sunflowers— usually Russian sunflowers— became very popular to grow in this time period, as the demand was growing for bird food due to the public's awareness of and love of bird watching. The area now houses the Frost Farm condominium complex.

Frank H. and Lauretta Hadley sit outside their house at 308 Concord Road in Sudbury Center. Frank H. Hadley was a retired railroad man. Lauretta is dressed in a costume for the town's 300th anniversary in 1939.

Two

PEOPLE A TO Z

This is a lovely portrait of Ruth Ames. She was born in 1899, never married, and was the last owner of the Ames Farm, originally consisting of 150 acres at 37 Landham Road. She was famous for her pies and she funded the Ames Hall at the Memorial Congregational Church.

Elizabeth Atkinson was the town librarian at the Goodnow Library from 1937 to 1970. She lived with her sister at 85 Raymond Road in a house built in 1826 by Jonas Hunt for his son Sewell Hunt. Atkinson was highly regarded and loved by townspeople, especially by their children, as she paid special attention to the shy children who needed assistance in learning how to enjoy reading. The society has a collection of artistic photographs taken of her in her house with her Great Dane.

Baseball legend Babe Ruth, his daughter Dorothy, and their dogs pose in front of their home in Sudbury. In 1923, he bought the Obadiah Perry farm at 558 Dutton Road, built in 1800, and renamed it Home Plate. In 1927, it was sold to Herbert and Esther Atkinson, who started a company in the barn called Sudbury Labs, making everything from soil-testing kits to invisible boats. The Atkinsons also created the Sudbury Foundation, a local charity that has done much for Sudbury and the surrounding area.

Babe Ruth (above) became a gentleman farmer in Sudbury, and for a few years, it was his place to relax, especially in the winter. Here, he helps his daughter Dorothy feed the chickens in a planned photograph opportunity for the visiting press, who made many demands on him. The son of the home's current owners claims to have broken the Red Sox "Curse of the Bambino" when he was hit by a fly ball in 2004 at Fenway Park. Later that year, the Red Sox won the World Series for the first time since Ruth was infamously traded to the Yankees.

Loring Coleman, shown at right, is a well-known artist in New England. Born in 1918 in Chicago, he is a descendant of Rev. Jacob Bigelow, an early minister in Sudbury. He spent summers at his grandmother's house in Concord, where he filled his sketchbooks with drawings. Boarding school brought him back to Massachusetts, where painting became his passion as he moved from oils to watercolors. Coleman has taught at Vesper George School in Boston and Middlesex School in Concord and was the supervisor of art programs for Sudbury schools. (Photograph by Hugh Portmiller.)

The watercolor above shows the Forrest D. Bradshaw store, which once occupied 361 Boston Post Road opposite Concord Road, next to where Mill Village is now. The Bradshaws bought the store in 1921. The original owner, Enoch Kidder, built it in 1820 and made shoes and boots. The second floor was the meeting place for local abolitionists and the location of the founding of the Sudbury Republican party. The watercolor is by Sudbury artist Loring Coleman. (Reprinted with permission by the owner, Dr. Donald Oasis.)

Forrest D. and Katherine Rogers Bradshaw pose under a painting of the South Sudbury railroad station, which now hangs in the Goodnow Library. Forrest was a World War I veteran who served in the Balloon Observation Corps. In addition to running his general store, he loved town history and was the town historian and a founder of the Sudbury Historical Society, Inc. He also found time to be a town selectman while he was also the Sudbury postmaster.

Auxiliary officer Lloyd Bancroft and his 1943 Hudson automobile were ready for duty. The Bancroft family lived at 277 Old Sudbury Road in what was known as the Harrington Place. Bancroft was a full-time baker of bread and rolls in his own bakeshop on the property. The baked goods were delivered to local restaurants and clients. The family won fifth place in a contest as the "Most Typical American Family in Massachusetts" in 1939.

This formal portrait of the Cutler family in the mid-1930s includes, from left to right, Mary Edith Goodnow Cutler, Richard Thompson Cutler, Isadora Goodnow Cutler, Philip Loring Cutler, Edward Roland Cutler, Joseph Stone Cutler, Roland Rogers Cutler Jr., and Roland Rogers Cutler Sr. Their middle names reveal connections to other longtime residents of the community, such as Goodnow, Loring, Rogers, and Stone. The Cutlers live on Landham Road.

John H. Eaton was born on November 17, 1838, in Sudbury. He lived here his whole life and worked as a carpenter, never marrying. In 1910, he was living with his sister Sarah Butterfield and was also the brother of Edward and Newell Eaton. The Eaton family still lives in Sudbury today.

Frank H. Hadley fills up his pail at his pump in the town center around 1920. Hadley used to offer passing residents a cool drink from his well. The pump was renovated by the current owner. The superbly restored and maintained house is located at 308 Concord Road in the Sudbury Center Historic District.

Herbert Frost, dressed in his good straw hat and vest, carries his watering can on April 27, 1915, at his home at 47 Concord Road, which is known as the Richard Rush Horr House. The monument in the background was perhaps in the nearby Wadsworth Cemetery, where he could have been watering flowers.

The Goodnow family proudly poses in front of their farm at 163 Landham Road, which was built from 1884 to 1886. The photograph was taken in 1888, showing the barn, which was constructed before the house, and the house, when it was a simpler Queen Anne style. Windmills were a common sight in that day. They used the wind to pump up water from a well to a holding tank in the attic of the house or barn, sometimes both, after which gravity would deliver it to indoor plumbing or to watering troughs for the animals.

Lillian Hunt (left) and Hattie Goodnow (third from the left) pose above with two other unidentified Hunt relatives. Goodnow was a photographer who took many photographs of her family and the Sudbury area in all kinds of weather. When the Griswolds purchased her house at 293 Concord Road, they gave the historical society Goodnow's camera and glass-plate negative slides.

Baby Edgar Goodnow and three-year-old Edward Cookson smile for the camera. Another founding family of Sudbury, the Goodnows left their mark on Sudbury when John Goodnow donated a public library in 1863. The Goodnow Reunion Group is very active and even goes back to England occasionally on tours.

Edgar W. Goodnow was dressed for a formal occasion, complete with a waxed handlebar moustache. His son Edgar W. Goodnow Jr. lived at 10 Hudson Road in the 1802 Joel Moore House until he passed away recently.

On a hot summer day, Ruth Goulding took this photograph of, from left to right, her brother-in-law Bill Goulding, Frank Taylor, George W. Hunt, and Leonard Goulding, with his Springer Spaniel. The Gouldings ran a very successful antique business at 88 Concord Road, and Henry Ford was a good customer. Leonard Goulding used to strip the antique finish off his pieces in the yard behind the house, which explains why nothing grows there.

Sudbury artist Florence Hosmer (1880–1978) holds a book with her family listed in it. She was a professional portrait artist of prominent people and painted over 500 known works. She studied at Massachusetts Normal Art School and the Boston Museum School as well as with other notable painters. She exhibited at the Copley Society of Art and the Boston Art Club. A recent book, *My Dear Girl*, was written about her life and her art by Sudbury author Helen Marie Casey.

Hosmer House is located at 299 Old Sudbury Road at the corner of Concord Road. It was originally built in 1793 by Elisha Wheeler and was bought in 1897 by Edwin Hosmer. Hosmer's daughter Florence a noted artist in her time, deeded the house to the town in memory of her father and her brother in 1959, with the provision that she could live there and the town would take care of her until her death.

Sudbury resident William Haynes, seen here on April 25, 1901, worked as an officer at the Charlestown prison. He was later presented with a special song called "Oh Charlestown, Oh Charlestown" by its lyrical composer E.M. Dana and musical composer Leroy J. Pierce. It was sung at a minstrel show on February 24 and 25, 1919.

A young Harry Hunt finishes up a woodworking project in the new woodworking shop in the basement of the new high school, which now houses town offices and is called the Flynn or White Building. He was a member of one of Sudbury's early families, and his aunt Hattie Goodnow took this photograph of him.

Lillian Goodnow Hunt, the mother
of Harry Hunt, posed in costume
to emulate a classic painting
for her sister Hattie Goodnow.
(Photograph by Hattie Goodnow.)

Bill Hanley lived in the King Philip
neighborhood in 1917 and did odd jobs. He
was willing to work hard, and as these were
his normal work clothes, his wife was not shy
about asking him to shovel coal or whatever
was needed, as he could not get any dirtier.
(Photography courtesy of Harriet Richardson.)

Leona Johnson stands by a fireplace in her home at 301 Old Lancaster Road. Note the tags on the two jugs—she marked everything in her house as to where it would go when she passed away. As the town archivist, she not only saved everything but also did so in an orderly way. One could ask her to find anything and off she would go to one of her antique trunks and pull it out. She kept scrapbooks of different pieces of Sudbury history, which are now at the Goodnow Library and at the town clerk's office.

This Klansman is one of the men in the Oliver family, either Reginald, Basil, or grandfather Horace. The photograph was taken at 623 Peakham Road and donated by Linda L. Muri. The KKK had made inroads in Sudbury in the early 1920s due to unrest about the separation of church and state, Prohibition, and the influx of new ethnic groups. It culminated on August 9, 1925, with more than 150 men assembled at the Libbey Farm off Landham Road. After the armed men rioted, the state police had to be called in. In all, 75 men were arrested and 24 were tried. The judge warned them that they had the right to assemble but not to bear arms, and he essentially dropped the case.

An 1893 Wadsworth School class poses in front of the school, which was on the site of current police station at 415 Boston Post Road. The towns did not hire married schoolteachers until after World War II. These two teachers shown are Marion Eaton (second row, seated) and Jennie Hunt (rear). The teachers' common complaint back then regarded the animal odor of the students in close quarters.

These lovely ladies in their Sunday best in 1919 were, from left to right, Ella Oviatt, Lottie Smith, and Harriet Goodnow after they attended a service at Memorial Congregational Church. Oviatt was married to Dr. George A. Oviatt, and they lived at 394 Boston Post Road. Smith was the aunt of Curt Garfield, who was a published author on birds and horticulture and the town historian and lived at 106 Woodside Road. Harriet Goodnow lived at 4 King Philip Road.

When Hattie Goodnow took this picture, she made a living as a teacher in the communities of Sudbury, Weymouth, and Newton, seen here in 1902. Either this was a special dress-up day or Newton folks dressed their children very well.

Harry Rice stands in the doorway of Broadmeadow Stable, which was once at 130 Water Row near Plympton Road. He is guarding two family muskets. The one on the left was made by H. Sleur. It is called a fowler and was carried to Concord by Ezekiel Rice on April 19, 1775. The second one was made by Thomas Holbrook. Through the generosity of an SHS member, the Rice musket was donated and is on exhibit at the National Heritage Museum in Lexington.

This photograph of the 1787 Rice-Haynes-Smith homestead at 130 Water Row was taken about 1870. The house was carefully torn down in 1981 by Charles and Ann Orr and put in storage until it was lovingly rebuilt at 137 Plympton Road. Standing in the photograph are two members of the Smith family and their farmhand. Around 1810, it was sold to Benjamin Smith, whose daughter married into the Rice family. Three generations later, Harry Rice, the last family member to live there, was born.

This close-up photograph shows the Rice-Haynes-Smith homestead in the 1870s. The Smith ladies are wearing their Sunday best, complete with hoop skirts and bustles, which were very stylish at the time. The hired hand in the background kept the farm running. The Rice family has been in Sudbury since the 1600s.

Artist and schoolteacher Gertrude "Lizzie" Rice relaxes outdoors. She was related to one of the founding families of Sudbury and lived from 1877 to 1960. She enjoyed sketching wildflowers throughout the area. Between 1915 and 1920, she sketched more than 180 flowers with colored pencils in a notebook, which is in the SHS collection. She lived at 328 Goodman's Hill Road, which was later owned by the famed calligrapher and illuminator E. Helene Sherman.

This daylily drawing was done by Gertrude Rice in 1916. Rice enjoyed roaming around Sudbury in her buggy drawn by her faithful horse, Old Guy, or on her bike, to different fields, brooks, woods, and swamps to capture wildflowers with colored pencils. She had no training, but her flowers speak volumes with their careful attention to detail. The Sudbury Historical Society sells full-color note cards of three of her images.

Phil Richardson rides in his wicker baby carriage in 915. A member of another founding Sudbury family, young Phil was doted on and is seen in several period pictures from when he was a baby to when he joined the Coast Guard in World War II. The Richardson homes are in South Sudbury on King Philip Road.

This is a portrait of Henry Smith, a commercial flower grower around 1900 who also packaged seeds. He sold the seeds through his own catalog and was innovative in his growing of popular flowers, collecting the seeds, and packaging them attractively. Henry developed the very popular present-day Cosmos flower from a wild, late-blooming Cosmos. Smith was the grandfather of the former town historian, Curt Garfield, and lived at 106 Woodside Road and 94 Woodside Road.

E. Helene Sherman was a remarkable artist who was born in Wayland in September 1908. Her family had a long artistic background and her first teacher was her maternal grandfather, noted French painter Edmond Prang, the cofounder of the Prang Company, well-known color printmakers around 1900. She learned her lettering in art school and taught herself illumination. She studied at the Pierpont Morgan Library in New York City, at the Boston Public Library, at the Huntington Library in California, in Paris, and in the Archives of the Vatican in Rome. Her illuminated paintings, miniature books, and bas-relief art are exhibited in several locations all over the world, including the National Archives.

I HEARD
a bird sing in the
dark of December
A magical thing and
sweet to remember,
"We are nearer to
Spring ~ than
we were in September."
I heard a bird sing in
the dark of December.
OLIVER HERFORD.

This is an example of illumination by E. Helene Sherman, a nationally known calligrapher and manuscript illuminator as well as watercolorist. Illumination is an ancient profession dating from the first century AD. Most of the completed works were done by cloistered monks on religious texts. Later, in the 12th century, the "first initial" decoration was developed, which included raised and burnished gold and detailed miniatures within the letter itself. The SHS has a collection of her works.

Rex Trailer (left), a Sudbury resident and local celebrity, is seen here with Jerry Lewis raising funds for the Muscular Dystrophy Association. Trailer was a real cowboy and hosted a Boston and Baltimore television show called *Boomtown* from 1956 to 1974. In 2012, as "the cowboy with a conscience," Trailer was named the Official Cowboy of Massachusetts. This photograph was taken for WBZ-TV on May 15, 1969.

Shown below, from left to right, Sam Underwood, Percival "Dad" Jones, and John Goulding sit in front of the Goulding House at 88 Concord Road. The house was originally in Wayland and known as the Moses Brewer House, before it was moved to this spot and reassembled from 1919 to 1925. It was then opened as an antique shop by Leonard Goulding.

This Wadsworth Academy class included, from left to right, (first row) Dana Whiting, Oscar Morris, Alvin Noyes , Robert Taft, Frankie Adams, Maxwell Eaton, Elmond Garfield, Frank Taft, and Francis Kennedy; (second row) Fred Chamberlain, Ralph Wilson, Laurice Rogers, Margaret Taft, Erskin Rogers, Elizabeth Atkinson, Alberto Stone, Hope Whitney, and Elbridge Whitney; (third row) Fordis Garfield, Robert Atkinson, Clarence Chickering, teacher Loren P. Burke, Marie Fisher, Mary Adams, and Ralph Eaton. The school was located at 26 Concord Road before it burned in 1879. The Memorial Congregational Church occupies that site now.

This 1930s classroom was at the South School, found at 29 Massasoit Avenue in South Sudbury. Included in this photograph, in no particular order, are Robert Walker, Phil Richardson, Phil and Annie Cutler, Erica Johnson, Sally Perry, Charlotte Whitworth, Dean Honks, and Earl Hoyle. The group may also have included Ruth Way, Patsy Mercury, George Duane, Ruth Stone, and Paul Carr. The SHS has one desk from this school in its collection.

Sudbury
HIGH SCHOOL
Class of 1950

Eloise Burr · Louise Richardson · Louise Pride · Madeline Quinn · Edith Smith · Shirley Kahilainen

William Schofield · Robert Johnson

Richard Eaton · George Gennato

James Poole
President

Lawrence Storey, Jr.
Vice President

Marcia Gaughan
Secretary

Anne Burns
Treasurer

The Sudbury High School class of 1950 went to school in what is now the Flynn or White Building at 278 Old Sudbury Road. Only 14 students graduated that year, six years before the new Lincoln Sudbury Regional High School opened.

The Center School was built in 1891 as a combined grammar school and the area's first high school. The design was so well thought of that it was entered in a World's Fair competition. It served as the high school through the 1953–1954 school year. Currently housing town offices, it is now known as the Flynn Building, named for Alan Flynn, a beloved principal of the high school, or the White Building.

46

Three
CELEBRATIONS

Sudbury residents are seen in front of the First Parish Church dressed up as Puritans for the celebration of the 300th anniversary of the town in 1939. There were recreations of church services, town meetings, singing, and historic speeches. Only 56 individuals and families began the settlement in 1639 on the other side of the Sudbury River in what is now Wayland.

In 1939, Frank H. Hadley stood out in front of his house at 308 Concord Road and personally thanked every participant and vehicle in the 1930 Fourth of July Parade, offering them a drink of his cold, pure well water. Nowadays in the parade, by the time marchers get to this house, Boy Scouts and Girl Scouts have probably offered them bottled water, but it must have tasted great back then.

The family of Samuel B. Rogers turned their horse and buggy into a parade float in 1926 to celebrate the country's 150th birthday. Sudbury loves parades, and the Fourth of July Parade continues to be one of the biggest around, supported by the chamber of commerce. Unfortunately, fireworks are no longer set off behind the Flynn Building.

48

This wagon stops in front of Hunt's Store at 356 Boston Post Road in 1915 and is ready to join the Fourth of July Parade. The children are dressed in their Sunday best, and some of the boys are wearing Civil War caps. Sudbury had several African American families, beginning with the Morris family, who lived at 253 Concord Road. (Photograph by Harriet Richardson.)

The town of Sudbury enjoys the parade in 1915. A Model T Ford waits to enter the parade, with a horse and buggy behind it. The parade used to start at Massasoit Avenue. Harriet Richardson took this photograph on the Boston Post Road opposite No. 353.

Dominion Day, seen here in 1914, was hosted by Raymond's Department Store owner Canadian-born George J. Raymond and his wife, Lydia, at the Raymonds' Sudbury estate at 80 Raymond Road. Raymond stands to the left with a young lady in white on either side of him. This holiday celebrates the confederation of Canada on July 1 and is now known as Canada Day.

George J. Raymond watches his toy bulldog. The Raymonds moved into their 500-acre estate in 1903, making several additions to the house and adding extensive gardens over several cultivated acres.

Temperance Oakes Guptill poses in the entrance to the gazebo on the Raymond estate, with more than five acres of flowers, bushes, and trees cared for by five full-time gardeners and much part-time help on the 500-acre estate. Guptill was a strikingly handsome woman even into her late years. Participants in the Raymond parties were always encouraged to come in ethnic costumes like hers.

George Raymond was known to be theatrical, and skits were a part of the Dominion Day celebrations. Here, Frank I. Dorr holds the paddle as these rowdy partygoers attempt to row a canoe through the grass. Interestingly, the Algonquin name for the Sudbury River is Musketaquid, meaning "grassy ground." Dorr would later become the president of the Raymond's Department Store syndicate and have even bigger parties at his estate in Framingham.

Creating the town bonfire are, from left to right, (halfway up) Lawrence B. Tighe, Ray Phelps, and Myron Siegars; (at top) town firefighter J. Leo Quinn and Leonard Stiles. Looking closely, there is a rag doll monkey at the top. In 1934, the bonfire was built near where the Peter Noyes School is now located. (Photograph by Harriet Ritchie.)

Below, a 1930s Kayopha girls' camp gathered for their summer photograph here in Sudbury as a part of the Congregational Church's outreach program for girls. Kayopha is a Native American word that translates to "where the sky and the peaks touch."

Elizabeth Atkinson (left) and Marion Raymond Lundberg, George J. Raymond's daughter, are dressed as Puritan ladies for Sudbury's 1939 tercentennial. They are standing in front of the milk shed at the Raymond estate. Marion Lundberg served as president of the Sudbury Historical Society in the 1970s.

Lloyd and Kay Bancroft and their children, from left to right, Fred, Patty, and Lloyd Jr. pose in front of their house on Concord Road near Plympton Road. They are all dressed up for the 1939 tercentennial. The Bancroft family had deep roots in Sudbury and added to every occasion in which they participated.

This very young couple is seen driving a sparkling new model car in the 1976 Fourth of July Parade.

The parade for the tercentennial in September 1939 is seen here with Lloyd Bancroft riding on top of the coach dressed as a Native American. Bancroft seemed to be everywhere that day.

This Tom Thumb wedding at the Memorial Congregational Church in 1946 married Jane Flynn to Lloyd Bancroft Jr. John Hall was the minister, Fred Bancroft (far right) was a groomsman, and Patty Bancroft (back row, far left) was a bridesmaid. Tom Thumb weddings, based on the nuptials of Gen. Tom Thumb, who worked in the circus for P.T. Barnum in 1863, were popular, fashionable, and fun.

Dressed as a Native American but also wearing sunglasses because of the bright Fourth of July sun, Lloyd Bancroft led part of the 1939 parade through Sudbury. A great baker, Bancroft was a fun-loving gentleman who was very active in the town.

Forrest Bradshaw (left) shakes hands with selectman Harvey Fairbank, with selectman Laurence Tighe on the right. They are accepting the gift of a recreated set of stocks from the Sudbury Historical Society, Inc., which were set on the town common on May 18, 1957. Stocks were a way of punishing a person with public embarrassment and humiliation. These were destroyed by a school bus in 1968. (Photograph by Harriet Ritchie.)

These children have outfitted their bikes for the annual Fourth of July bike-decorating contest. This contest is still run on the Fourth of July, usually by the American Legion Post No. 191. This photograph was taken for the July 19, 1972, Sudbury Citizen newspaper by editor Mary Jane Hillery. At the time, there were two Sudbury newspapers, plus Bentley's Calendar, a weekly magazine.

The Sudbury Women's Club had this American pie sale on the town common on the Fourth of July to benefit their scholarship fund. The women participating included, from left to right, Lou Cali, Carol Bowman, Peggy Feistkorn, Lee Hamill, Ann Pettigrew, and Frances Schlichter.

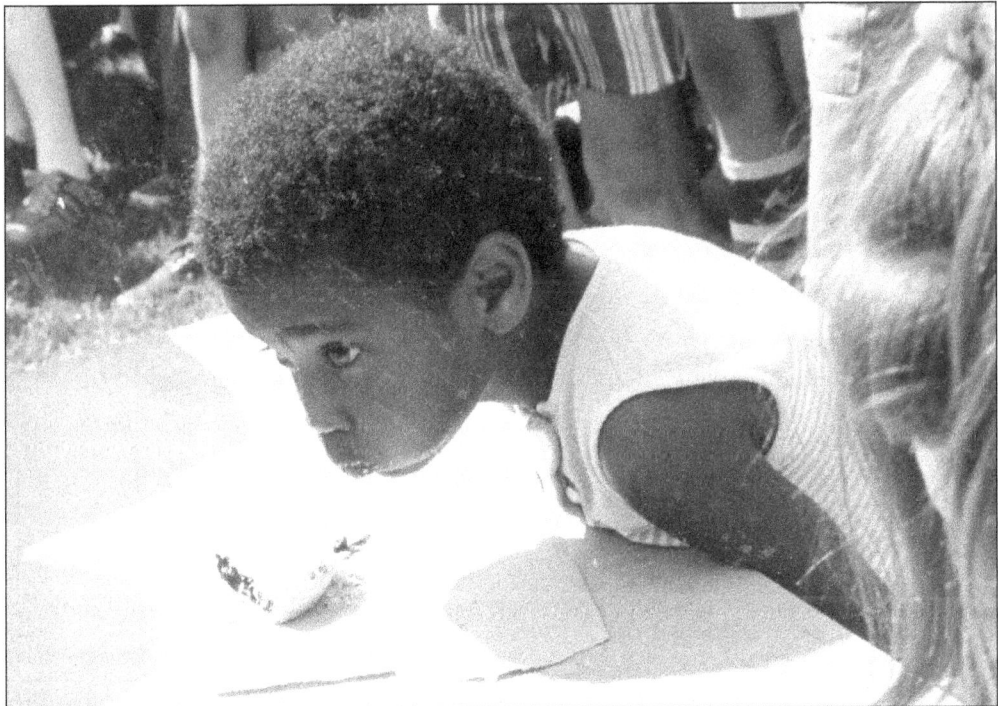

Casey Nolan finds his last bite tough going in the pie-eating contest at the 1972 Fourth of July celebration. This contest was usually held in the Peter Noyes field after the parade. (Photograph by *Sudbury Citizen*.)

The circus at the Peter Noyes School, seen here on August 13, 1970, was sponsored by the Sudbury police as a fundraiser for charity. At least two carnivals and a circus passed through town every year, aglow at night with strange sounds, sights, smells, and adventures. (Photograph by *Sudbury Citizen*.)

The 1968 Masquerade Parade at the Featherland playground included, from left to right, (first row) Terrie Bierig, Cheryl Slomski, and Clay Booma; (second row) Bobby Bierig, Robin Slomski, Missy Clark, and Alison Booma; (third row) Jason Doyle, Brian Bierig, Donna Roessler, Andrea Roessler, and Gretchen Booma. (Photograph by P. Brown for the *Sudbury Citizen*.)

A Leaping Lena clown car performs for the crowd during the 1968 Fourth of July Parade on Concord Road. This was a paid attraction sponsored by a local company as part of the Sudbury Chamber of Commerce parade.

The Wayside Inn stagecoach—before it was restored—drove through the Marlborough tercentennial in June 1960. Stagecoaches ran on the Post Road west from Boston to Marlborough and beyond. The passengers included Forrest and Katherine Bradshaw, Maud Clark, Elizabeth Atkinson, and Linda and Holly Peterson. The Walker Building is on the left, and Immaculate Conception Church is on the right.

This funny parade float in 1968 included the following joke: "Twas an old woman – lived in a shoe / Had so many kids – didn't know what to do / . . . so she moved to Sudbury." The joke was a commentary on the increased number of families moving to Sudbury at the time.

Below, the restored Wayside Inn stagecoach carried innkeeper Francis Koppeis and others in the 1975 Fourth of July Parade. The Abbot and Downing coach was restored by the fundraising of the Sudbury Companies of Militia and Minute and is now on display in the Collings Museum in Stow. It is still used at the end of the Sudbury Fourth of July parade every year.

This Fourth of July 1976 Parade float was sponsored by Mullen Lumber Company and featured a replica of the Redstone Schoolhouse with enthusiastic students.

This 1976 parade float passes by town hall in the center of Sudbury. The float encouraged people to vote and was likely sponsored by the League of Women Voters.

This early meeting of the Sudbury Companies of Militia and Minute took place at the Old Bar in the Wayside Inn in 1965. The late innkeeper, Francis Koppeis, was always a perfect host and helped start the recreated Minute Company and the Fife and Drum Corps. The meeting included, from left to right, (seated) Bob Oram, Roger Bump, John Palutchco, David Bentley, and Paul MacNally; (standing) Russ Kirby, Ira Amesbury, Bob McLean Sr., and an unidentified British spy.

Mrs. Charles (Marion) Spiller (left) was the parade marshal of the 1973 Memorial Day Parade. She is dressed with her American Legion Post No. 191 cap and is pinned with a corsage. Spiller was a Gold Star Mother—someone who lost a son in World War II—for having lost her son Albert. The Memorial Day Committee plans a year in advance how to honor those who fought for their country. (Photograph by Clay Allen for the *Sudbury Citizen*.)

Four

SACRED SPACES

The first meetinghouse and church in Sudbury was built in what is now the North Cemetery in Wayland on Old Sudbury Road, where the honored dead were buried around the church. This location served as the site of three different meetinghouses until the center of Wayland was reestablished at Route 20 and Route 126/27. A.S. Hudson, who wrote *The History of Sudbury*, painted this based on what he was told it looked like.

The First Parish Church in Sudbury's town center was originally built by journeymen builders in 1723 on what was known as Rocky Plain. The present structure was built in 1797 and reused some of the material from the original, smaller structure. The building's design was purchased from Benjamin Thompson of Boston and features design elements borrowed from famed English architect Christopher Wren. Town meetings were held here until 1846, when the town house was built and the separation of church and state was recognized.

This rare photograph of the interior of the First Parish Church was taken in 1904 by Hattie Goodnow. Originally, church services here were five hours long with a lunch break in the middle. There was no heat in the church, so members went to warm up by the fire in a nearby building called a noon house. To the right is the 1875 pump organ that was originally powered by a young man pumping a lever up and down during the service.

These are the gravestones of Rev. Jacob Bigelow and his wife, Elizabeth, in the Revolutionary War Cemetery. The family had the original inscribed-slate stones laid flat and had placed fashionable new vertical marble schist monuments in front of them. Sadly, the schist is greatly affected by acid rain, and the inscription on the slate is almost unreadable. Reverend Bigelow was ordained on November 11, 1772, as the minister at First Parish, succeeding Rev. Israel Loring after his death.

The Wadsworth Memorial Monument in Wadsworth Cemetery is opposite 71 Concord Road. It was named after Capt. Samuel Wadsworth, a militiaman from Milton. Captain Wadsworth and most of his company were attacked and killed while defending the frontier at the Battle of Green Hill. They fought the Native Americans during the King Philip's War on April 21, 1676. The first slate marker to identify the gravesite of the 26 militiamen and three officers who were killed was erected in 1730 by Wadsworth's son. In 1852, the 21.5-foot-tall granite obelisk was erected, and the cemetery was named in honor of Wadsworth.

The Cram Chapel is located in front of Ralph Adams Cram's home, Whitehall, at 435 Concord Road. Cram described it as a simple country chapel built for his private use. This Medieval-style building was constructed by hand, largely by local Sudbury craftsmen, including renowned ironworker Samuel Yellen, who built the fine iron strap-work, the lock on the doors, and components of the interior.

At left, Cram's daughter Mary Cram Carrington prays in Cram Chapel in 1902. The chapel was deeded to St. Elizabeth's Episcopal Church and used by the congregation until a much larger church was built nearby. The chapel is still used for summer services.

The Crams, standing at the Cram Chapel entrance, lived on the property, primarily in the summer, from 1900 to 1942. The couple is buried next to the chapel. The Crams owned a house in the city but were not unique in discovering the pleasures of a country town, especially after the arrival of the railroads in the 1870s, after which well-to-do men could live in Sudbury and travel to the city easily.

Ralph Adams Cram, who lived here, at Whitehall, was America's foremost ecclesiastical architect. He was internationally famous for his reinterpretation of the Gothic style of architecture and for incorporating it into modern structures. His most famous work was the Cathedral Church of Saint John the Divine in New York City.

Memorial Congregational Church at 26 Concord Road is seen here in 1944. The church was built in 1889 and dedicated on March 8, 1891. Today, it is well known for its annual Messiah Sing in December, which everyone is invited to participate in. It occupies the previous site of the Wadsworth Academy.

The Memorial Congregational Church received this new organ in 1904. The interior has since been completely remodeled and rearranged. The photograph was taken by Hattie Goodnow, whose work chronicling the town through photographs likely made this book possible.

The Evangelical Union Society was located at 277 Concord Road across from Goodman's Hill Road. It was dedicated on January 1, 1840, by the Evangelical Union Society, when it split from the Unitarians in 1837. The congregation chose to erect a new church in 1889 at 26 Concord Road in South Sudbury. The building has since gone through many uses, first as a music hall and lastly as a home to a basketball league, before it burned in 1925. The present house at this address was moved onto the site from another location.

North Cemetery on Pantry Road features the statue shown at left, which is engraved with "Maynard" at its base. It is a very rare hollow zinc statue. In the 1830s, a John Maynard lived in Sudbury and is remembered for saying, "Everyone who called, from minister to tramp, was offered a common drink."

This Italian chapel was located on Mossman Road and built by the Maria SS. Indulgence Society, which was founded in 1914. The chapel itself was built in the 1920s, and society membership was limited to descendants of residents of the town of Sant' Elia Fiuma Rapido near Monte Cassino, Italy. The society functioned as a mutual aide society, providing health and unemployment benefits. However, as time passed, younger generations became disinterested. The chapel was torn down in 1988, and the land was sold for housing.

Every year on the third Sunday of July, members of the Maria SS. Indulgence Society carried over the tradition from Italy of the procession to the chapel for adoration of the Madonna. The statue was brought to the Micelli house on Route 117 the Thursday before and decorated with contributions from the devout. Mass was celebrated at the entrance to the stone chapel because the large crowd attending could not fit inside. The afternoon was spent with picnics, dancing, and family gatherings.

70

MARIA SS. DELLE INDULGENZE
a Cavooto family photo

This interior photograph of the Maria SS. Indulgence Society chapel shows the Madonna draped with traditional money offerings. Due to the limited size of the chapel, an outside area was created that was much like an amphitheater, with a roof under which as many as 30,000 people could assemble, including those who were seated, standing, and enjoying picnic lunches under the trees. John F. Kennedy visited the chapel to promote his senatorial campaign.

The Martha Mary Chapel was built in 1939 by students from the Wayside Inn Boys School, the Redstone Schoolhouse, and the South West School, assisted by local craftsmen. The craftsmen used the massive white pines that were downed by the 1938 hurricane to build the chapel, which was named after the mothers of Clara and Henry Ford. It is on the grounds of the Wayside Inn in the Wayside Inn Historic District. Since 1940, it has been the chapel of choice for 150 to 200 weddings a year. The chapel is a one-quarter-scale copy of the Bradford, Massachusetts, First Parish Chapel, and Henry Ford had five other similar chapels built wherever he had a school.

Five

MILITARY

This Old Town Bridge marker is on the original Route 27 beside the Wayland Country Club. It marks the place where eight Concord men died on April 22, 1676, while coming to Sudbury's aid during the King Philip's War. The names of the men, listed on the side, are as follows: James Hosmer, John Barnes, Samuel Potter, Daniel Comy, Joseph Butterick, David Curry, Josiah Wheeler, and William Hayward.

The Revolutionary Patriots Monument was dedicated on June 17, 1896, in honor of the soldiers and sailors of Sudbury who fought at Lexington, Concord, Bunker Hill, and in other battles of the Revolutionary War from 1775 to 1783. William Stone's father, Waldol, posed for the monument. One of the gentlemen who addressed the crowd that day was noted historian A.S. Hudson, who reported that out of the Sudbury population of 2,100, probably 500 were in the Concord and Lexington fights on April 19, 1775.

Below is the Revolutionary War Cemetery in Sudbury's town center. It was originally known as Ye Olde Burying Ground and began in 1716. At the time of the American Revolution, Sudbury was the largest town in Middlesex County.

This was a Memorial Day observance in front of Goodnow Library in 1980. The Civil War statue was erected in honor of those who fought from Sudbury. Doug Lewis is shown standing on the right, with Forrest Bradshaw, the town historian at the time, reading from his notes.

The Grand Army of the Republic (GAR) marches on Memorial Day 1916, turning the corner onto Concord Road. The GAR was a Civil War veterans group that banded together to fight for Veterans' rights. On this day, 10 Sudbury veterans marched or were driven. The SHS's remarkable collection of letters from Pvt. George F. Moor and his family (1862–1865) formed the basis of the SHS's new book, *From Your Loving Son*, in 2012. (Photograph by Harriet Richardson.)

This is the grave of Civil War veteran Samuel Bent Jr., who died on July 18, 1885. Bent, from an old Sudbury family, was a farmer who was conscripted into the Civil War in 1863 at age 30. Every year for Memorial Day, all the graves of veterans are honored with flags placed in specific flag holders in their honor.

This postcard shows World War I soldier Maurice B. White in full uniform. White, a Sudbury youth, was stationed at Fort Myer, Virginia, in May 1918 attached to the 37th Engineering Corps of Company D. The postcard was sent to the Richardson family on King Philip Road. Luckily, Sudbury did not lose any native sons in World War I.

American Legion Post No. 191 used to be located at 415 Boston Post Road, at the previous location of the Wadsworth School, which now houses the police department. Members of the post worked together to obtain the cannon shown above to decorate the front lawn. The World War I Italian field piece was obtained from the Framingham National Guard arsenal in 1926. Posing with the cannon are, from left to right, Forrest Bradshaw, Alfred F. Bonazzoli, Albert Tallant, and Maj. Dr. Albert Owen, who hauled it over with a Bonazzoli coal truck.

Sudbury twins Russell (left) and Robert Mugford are dressed in their World War II uniforms, which specify that they were in the honor guard at command headquarters in the Pacific Theater of the war. One of their duties was to drive and escort Gen. Douglas MacArthur.

Marine sergeant Leo Spottswood of Sudbury was photographed with his boot camp class at Norfolk, Virginia, on June 16, 1915, the same year he achieved marksman status. Spottswood was the father of local artist Joan Meenan.

Sergeant Spottswood is seen at right at the end of World War I, after he survived fighting in the trenches in France and was decorated with a Purple Heart and other ribbons. Later, as a civilian, he had the unique opportunity of driving Charles Lindbergh and his new wife, Anne Morrow, on their honeymoon in the United States.

Don Somers of Sudbury climbs into an SNJ fighter plane during basic flight training in the US Navy. Somers fought in the Korean War from 1950 to 1953. His wife, Nancy, is an SHS trustee.

This photograph shows the Raising of the Colors on Memorial Day 1972 at the flagpole in front of the town hall. From left to right are Doug Lewis of American Legion Post No. 191; Al Bonazzoli, formerly of the 26th Yankee Division; and Sgt. Leo Spottswood. Bonazzoli helped start the Sudbury Companies of Militia and Minute in 1962.

Sudbury local Phillip Richardson looks very happy in his Coast Guard uniform during World War II. As a child, he used to play being a soldier, sailor, or cowboy with his gang on King Philip Road. The SHS has been gifted with his uniforms along with much historical material from the Richardson family.

Maj. Herbert Hardy (left), of Normandy Drive in Sudbury, and Maj. Leslie Caufield, of Moore Road in Wayland, are seen with this Civil Air Patrol plane. In the late 1930s, more than 150,000 volunteers with a love for aviation argued for an organization to put their planes and flying skills to use in defense of their country. As a result, the Civil Air Patrol was born one week prior to the Japanese attack on Pearl Harbor.

Charles Pepper, of Sudbury, smiles broadly with his cleaned mess kit in his hand in Okinawa in 1944.

Preparing for a parade on Memorial Day 1998 are Sudbury veterans, from left to right, Don Somers, Charlie Pepper, Don Peirce, Lincoln Sudbury Regional High School student Mark Wyman, and Air Force colonel Clay Allen, who once displayed his medals, citations, and awards, which took up two full tables. Here, Colonel Allen still fits into his original dress uniform and marched in the parades into his 90s.

The above photograph of the 2nd Battalion, 26th Marines, 5th Division was taken on July 20, 1944 during training at Camp Pendleton in California. This is the middle portion of a three-foot panoramic picture and is believed to include an unidentified Sudbury boy. (Courtesy of Spencer Goldstein.)

This photograph of a Navy man and his fashionable wife was found in a wooden Commander Beverage case in Wellesley. The Commander Beverage Company operated from around 1900 up to the 1960s, initially on the eastern corner of the intersection of Boston Post Road and Union Avenue in Sudbury. In the 1930s, they moved into a new building at 621 Boston Post Road. (Courtesy of Doreen Kemp.)

Six

TRANSPORTATION

This photograph was posed at Longfellow's Wayside Inn in several variations in 1926 using one of the stagecoaches that late innkeeper Edward R. Lemon had collected. The purpose was to create a historical jigsaw puzzle. It was the start of the national craze for jigsaw puzzles, which continued unabated during and after the Great Depression. At the time, one could buy daily jigsaw puzzles at newsstands.

The Wayside Inn railroad waiting room was of a very stylish Japanese design and was built by the Boston & Maine Railroad in 1897. At the time, it was described as a cozy, comfortable depot. It was located on Dutton Road at the railroad track, and those inside had to flag down the trains themselves. Babe Ruth, Henry Ford, and guests of the inn all had to do just that. The building was burned by vandals in the 1940s, and its remains are no longer visible. (Courtesy of Robert Seymour.)

This is a very rare photograph taken at the 1910 Brockton Fair, where the world-famous aviator Alberto Santos-Dumont displayed his powered dirigible for the edification and wonder of the public. A caricature of Santos-Dumont appeared in the British *Vanity Fair* in 1899, showing this very same dirigible, No. 6. This photograph was taken by Harriet Richardson on one of her family's expeditions to other parts of the state.

In this 1913 photograph, a young girl is dressed all in white on the right and a boy rides a bicycle on the left. Behind them, a man works in the field where the village green is today at 29 Hudson Road.

This 1910 Hupmobile is parked at the intersection of Hudson and Peakham Roads. Behind the car is the Thomas Stearns House at 18 Hudson Road, and past the house is the First Parish Church. (Courtesy of Russell Stearns.)

Edward McLaughlin used to live at the end of Garrison House Lane near the Wayside Inn. He eventually sold his house and land to Henry Ford in the 1920s, but his house was still called the McLaughlin House by the boys' school and the inn employees. McLaughlin fancied a high-stepping horse that he would put through its paces on the dirt roads around the inn. This barn became one of Henry Ford's dairy barns.

It took the town a long time to purchase this 1930 International fire truck. There were two major fires in 1925, which led the town to appoint a fire committee to make recommendations on new equipment. In 1926, it was recommended that a pumper be purchased, but the idea languished until the town hall burned on February 5, 1930, spurring the town to form the fire department in 1931.

The Wayside Inn fire truck is seen here in 1934. It was a pumper, bringing water to the fire or drawing the water from a nearby well or pond. The inn property included 40 houses, barns, a gristmill, schoolhouses, a lumber mill, and lumberyards on its 2,995 nearly contiguous acres. Although the greatest fear was forest fires, the inn's most damaging fire began in the inn itself in 1955.

This view of Mount Nobscot looks south on Nobscot Road in 1904. The mountain had been almost entirely clear-cut for firewood and lumber. This is what the countryside all around Sudbury looked like at the time, as citizens raised crops and planted orchards, keeping an odd woodlot of fine chestnut for fence rails and black locust for fence posts or just firewood.

In 1916, Harry Baldwin was the stationmaster at the South Sudbury station across from 28 Union Avenue. He is shown here holding a small-bore rifle with a pheasant in his other hand. Years earlier, John Goulding had reintroduced pheasants into Sudbury. Harry Baldwin was Hope Baldwin's father.

Below, Jack McKinnon (left) and an unidentified merchant pose at an Old Time Value Days promotion in the 1950s. The McKinnons owned a market and then a liquor store in Sudbury for three generations. The store was originally located at 320 Boston Post Road and later moved to 450 Boston Post Road. This photograph was taken at the Wayside Inn, where they had borrowed a carriage for the promotion.

Miles's Express, a 1901 Ford with zany decorations and inscriptions, was created for the 1939 Tercentennial Parade and looks like it actually ran.

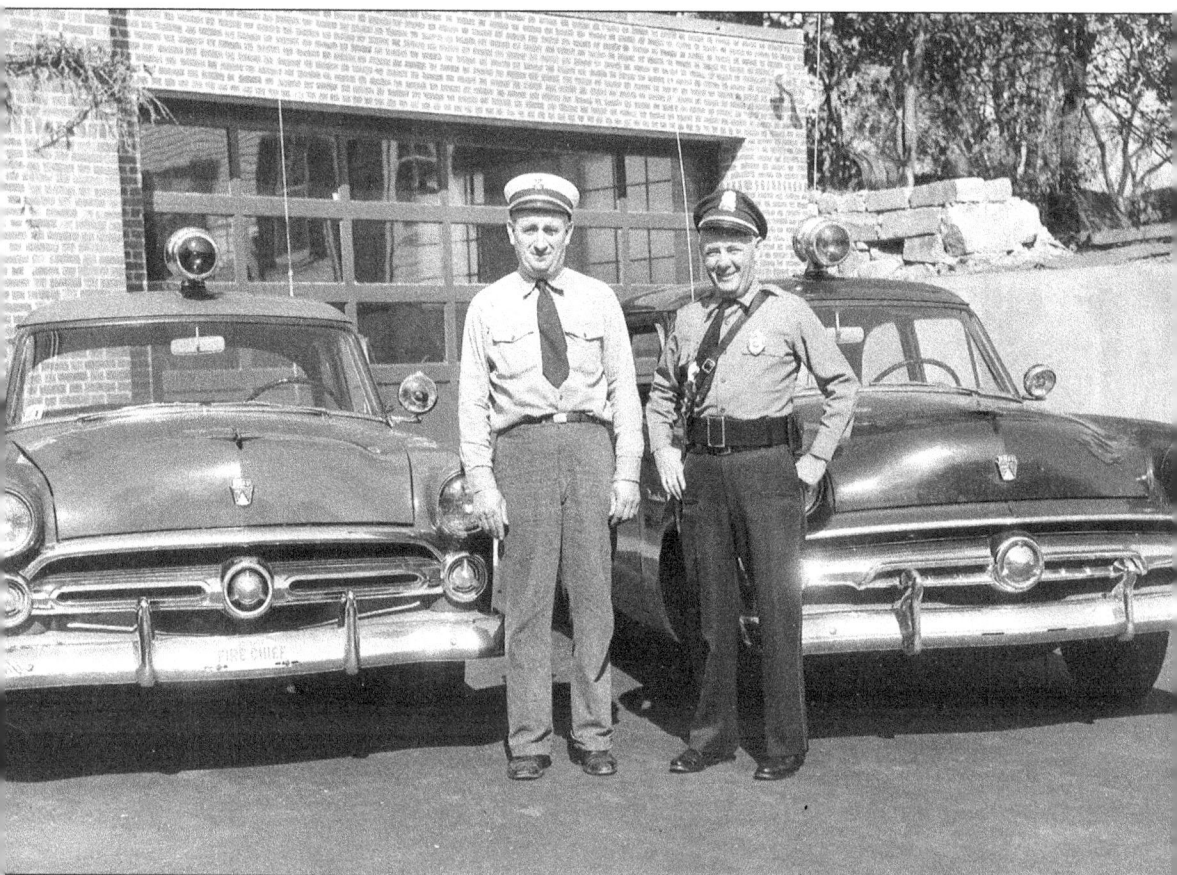

Sudbury fire chief Alfred St. Germain (left) and police chief John Mc Govern stand in front of their vehicles at the lower town hall fire station in 1954. The fire station, the town's first, was built in 1932.

Seven

RECREATION

This local lady posed for photographer Hattie Goodnow before a bicycle ride in 1904. Goodnow along with this woman and her identical sister, who were most likely schoolteachers, went camping at Eagle Camp in Vermont and other places. Sadly, Goodnow never wrote their names on the cardboard boxes that held her glass-plate negatives. (Photograph by Hattie Goodnow.)

Henry Smith (right) shows off his catch of brook trout with his employees after a summer day spent fishing at the Raymond farm pond, located on what is now near Warren Avenue. Smith lived at 106 Woodside Road and fished in this pond, which was never stocked—the fish were introduced by birds picking up fish eggs on their feet and transferring them. Note the glass of Smith's greenhouse in the background; he was quite the horticulturalist!

Helen Smith (left) and Lillie Lutz enjoy a summer day in a wooden canoe on the pond at the Raymond farm. They were relatives of Henry Smith who worked for him at the Cosmos Seed Company at 106 Woodside Road in 1910.

This young man, likely a Raymond heir, rides a tricycle in the early 1900s on the grounds of the Raymond estate.

Loretta Hunt plays a rough game of golf in a field that had just been hayed in 1902. The field was on Green Hill in Sudbury and belonged to the Goodnow family. (Photograph by Hattie Goodnow.)

E. Helene Sherman (left) and her sister Anna pose in their Girl Scout uniforms in 1920. Helene, who celebrated 65 years as a Scout in 1985, eked out a living as an artist specializing in illumination and calligraphy and went on to achieve fame with her works. She owned her house at 328 Goodman's Hill Road.

Unlike some baseball teams, the local team below actually had uniforms, which were usually supplied by a local business. The young man in front, James Bartlett, was the batboy. The partial list of names on this photograph includes, from left to right, (first row) Walter Carson, Ross ?, Patsy Mercury, John M., unidentified, and Charlie Whitworth; (second row) ? Whitney, unidentified, Lawrence Deroll, Jack Borden, Jack Giddings, and unidentified.

This baseball team and their coach line up for a team photograph in the late 1930s. Note the details of the early baseball glove at the bottom. This image also contains only a partial list of names, including, from left to right, (first row) Reynolds, Carson, two unidentified boys, George Duane, Norman Noyes, Bob Miller, and unidentified; (second row) Phil Richardson, unidentified, Patsy Mercury, Larry Hogan, James Deroll, Walter Stone, unidentified, and Little Joe Gleason.

These two coaches are formally dressed for the team photograph in the 1930s, taken for the *Green and White* commencement issue. The team included, from left to right, (seated) Ken Farrell, two unidentified boys, Al Clarke, unidentified, ? Lowell, and Patsy Mercury; (second row) unidentified, Loring Hogan, unidentified, Al Flynn, ? Lowell, Bob Miller, and Phil Richardson. The batboy is unidentified.

A group of explorers from the Algonquin Area Council went out to Minnesota for a canoe trip at the Wilderness Canoe Base. Only Roy Club (third row, far left), Curt Garfield (third row, second from right), and Dean Ram (third row, far right) were identified. The tradition continues today.

Brownie Troop No. 781 and their leaders pose at a local meeting. The year 2012 marked the 100th anniversary of the national Girl Scout organization.

These members of the Sudbury Players, seen here rehearsing *Footsteps of Doves*, are, from left to right, Carol Peskin, Guy Vincent, Ray Fawcett, and Judy Davis. In the 1960s, the group put on *You Know I Can't Hear You When the Water Is Running*.

The Sudbury Players were a local theater group who rehearsed and performed their plays on the second floor of the town hall until the Americans with Disabilities Act was passed in 1986. As there was no elevator in the town hall, the Sudbury Players had to look for other venues but could not afford the alternatives. In 1999, the Sudbury Historical Society was given the use of the second floor of town hall as a tenant-at-will. Only four of these players were identified; they are, in no particular order, Marshall Deutsch, Peter Sesen, Jim Moore, and Ginny Manzer.

The Sudbury Players are seen here rehearsing *Schubert*. They are, from left to right, (seated) Bette Cloud and Al Berberian; (standing) Ray Curran and Chris Childs.

The United Way campaign below was assisted by the local Boy Scouts and Girl Scouts posing here in front of the Wayside Inn in the 1970s.

Eight
AROUND TOWN

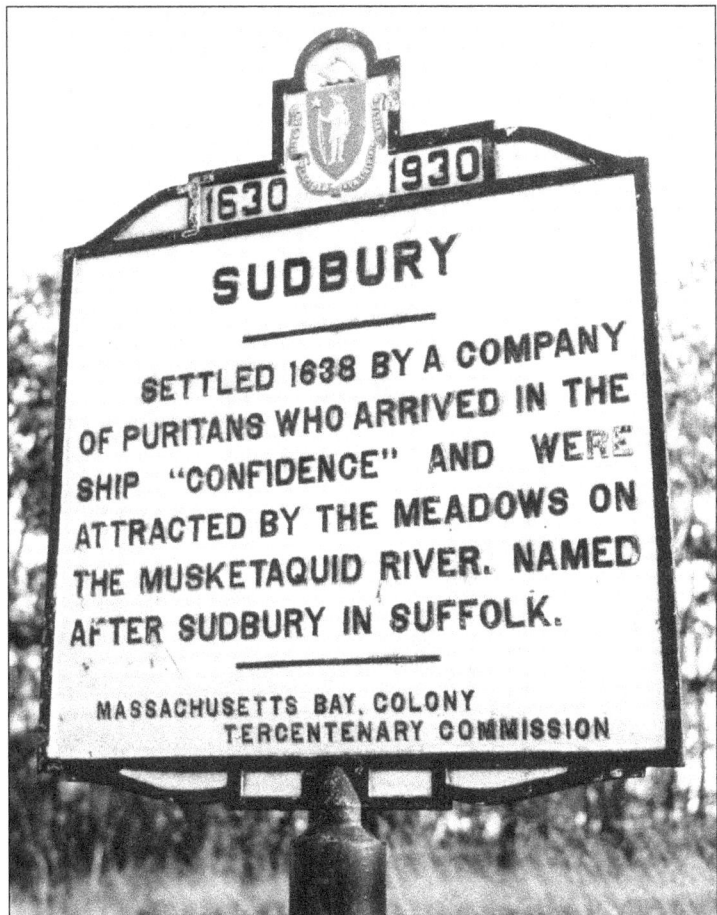

In 1930, the Massachusetts Bay Colony Tercentenary Commission created six markers for the town of Sudbury. The sign from the Marlborough entrance was stolen, while the marker at the Wayland entrance is still in place. The other markers noted historical sites in Sudbury such as the Goodnow Garrison.

The Indian grinding stone seen here sits on the southeast slope of Green Hill near the intersection of Singletary and Green Hill Roads. The boulder is six feet in diameter. The Nipmuc/Nipnet Native Americans ground corn, grains, and nuts into meal or flour against the indentation in the rock with a round stone. This mortar is unusually large but has a seat, as all of the other mortar stones in Sudbury do.

Goulding's Antique Shop, at 88 Concord Road, was originally known as the Moses Brewer House and was built in East Sudbury (now Wayland) on Route 27 around 1720. It was moved to its present location in 1918 by Leonard Goulding and restored to its original Saltbox style. The house has diamond-paned windows and a centered entrance. The contraption to the right side is known as a well sweep, which was used as a fulcrum to get water out of the well. The house is in the National Register of Historic Places.

Wooden footbridges were built here until 1643, when a wooden cart bridge was built to cross the Sudbury River. It was the primary connection between the settlements on the east and west sides of the river. Because the bridges washed away in the river so many times, it was continuously rebuilt over the next 143 years until 1866, when this fine stone bridge, which survives to this day, was built near 121 Old Sudbury Road in Wayland.

The Rice Tavern in the northwest district of Sudbury was built in the 1690s and served as a meeting place for many important selectmen and town meetings starting in the early 1700s. Many important decisions were made here to oppose the British crown and their taxes. It closed in 1815, but the Vose and Hunt family had a reunion there in 1880 when they owned it. The building's foundation still exists past the FEMA headquarters at the end of Old Marlborough Road off Route 27 in Maynard.

This 1896 photograph of Sudbury's town center is from a rare church calendar published by the Sudbury Methodist Episcopal Church. The church is the second building from the right, which was originally built as a Methodist church in 1836 and is now a Presbyterian church. On the right, the Sudbury Grange is hiding behind the town bandstand on the common. The building in the middle was the original town house, which was built in 1836 and burned in 1930.

The Adam Howe Jr. House is at the intersection of Wayside Inn Road at 882 Boston Post Road. The house was built by the son of the third innkeeper of the Red Horse Tavern (later known as the Longfellow's Wayside Inn). Built just before 1830 and remodeled between 1900 and 1915 with the addition of the columns and other improvements, the house still stands today.

The town pound was located on Concord Road next to the Revolutionary War Cemetery. Stray cattle, horses, sheep, and swine were kept and maintained by an official of the town called the pound keeper. A pound was first built in Sudbury around 1664, and this one was built in 1797 for $20. Another town official, the field driver, found the stray animals and drove them on foot to the pound. The recreated gate was made by the late Sam Reed of SHS in 1975.

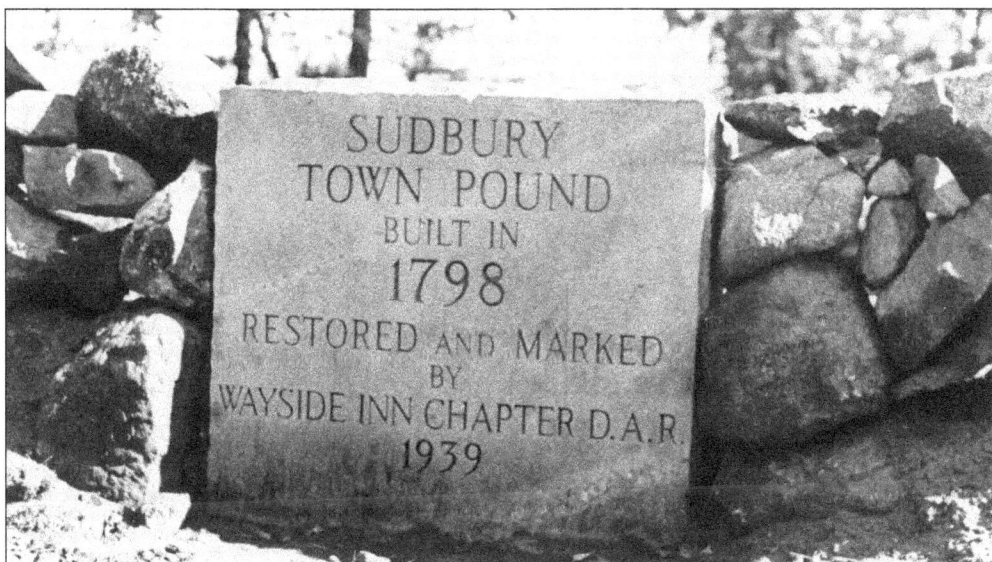

This marker denotes the Daughters of the American Revolution project to restore the town pound structure. They inserted the marker and made it part of the wall in 1939, after the restoration. A person driving by may think it is an unfinished foundation of a house, but it is not; it is one of only three known maintained town pounds in Massachusetts.

The original occupants of this unusual-looking house were Rev. Jacob Bigelow and his wife, Elizabeth. It was originally built in the Federalist style in 1773 and still stands at 250 Old Sudbury Road. Reverend Bigelow was hired by the town to serve as the minister. He had J. Thompson design and build the house. It was changed to look like this between 1900 and 1920.

The historic Walker House is located at 95 Peakham Road. Thomas Walker taught school for the town here and in other homes. In 1926, the house was restored by Henry Ford, who owned this and 40 other houses and buildings in the area. Its origins are somewhat of a mystery because none of the records from before Ford owned it still exist.

A gristmill and sawmill were located behind what is now the Mill Village shopping center. The Hurlbut and Rogers Machine Shop was also in the area. It has been a commercial center since 1659, when Peter Noyes and Abraham Wood built a gristmill on Hop Brook. By 1889, Mill Village consisted of a general store, a post office, a machine shop, a blacksmith, a schoolhouse, a church, a gristmill, a junction depot, the Goodnow Library, and 50 homes. It was considered quite progressive at the time.

C.O. Parmenter Gristmill and Sawmill was located on the Hop Brook around 1910. The mills were water-powered by undershot wheels. The water hit the wheels at the bottom to make them turn. The buildings have long since been torn down, and the area now serves as a parking lot for Mill Village.

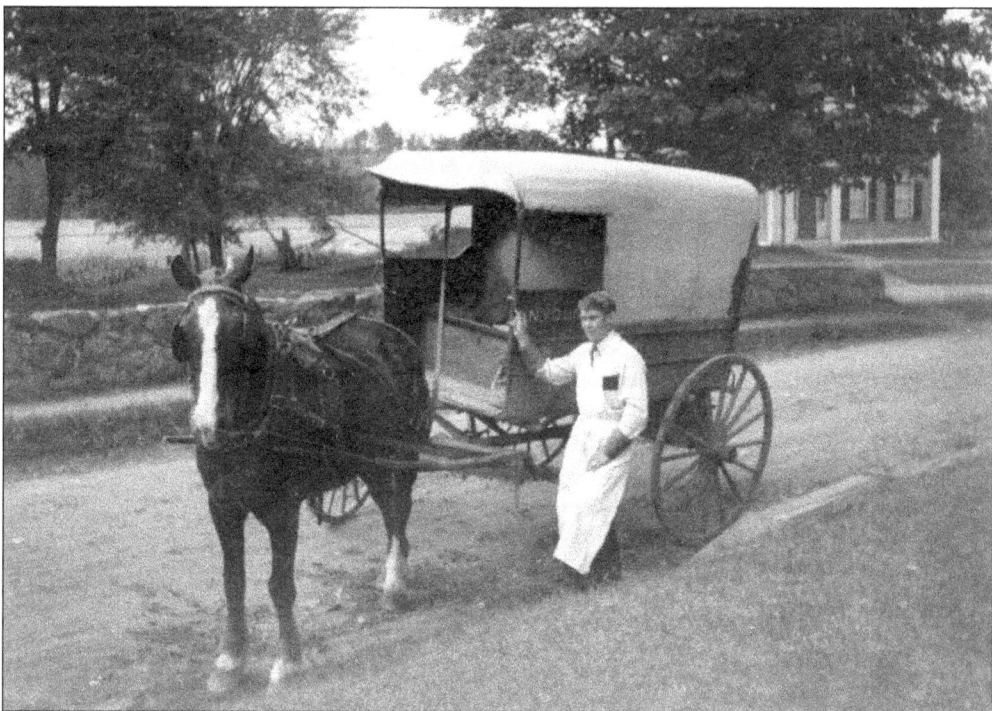

Everett M. Saunders holds up butcher Al Young's delivery wagon. In that time, orders were home delivered—Saunders would visit houses to take orders before going back to the store to pack the orders and deliver them.

The Sudbury Inn at 410 Boston Post Road was an old building that was not treated well through the years. It was reportedly built in the 1750s and was owned by the Wheeler family in 1830. In the 1920s, it was known as Ye Olde Barbeque Inn.

The famous "Old Kitchen" dining room at Longfellow's Wayside Inn is seen above in 1937. At the time, Henry Ford owned the inn and 2,995 acres around it. It was not a public dining area and could only be viewed on a paid tour. In 1945, on Ford's last visit to the inn before he died in 1947, he had 14 prominent industrialists to lunch in this room. Ford was known for his peculiar diet theories, but that particular lunch was especially befuddling to his guests.

This western view of the Wayside Inn was taken in 1885. The inn was on the Boston Post Road, which was originally called the Bay Path and King's Highway. When first licensed, it was called How's Inn or How's Tavern. The license allowed David How "to keep a house of entertainment for travelers," which meant he could serve alcohol and offer hospitality to strangers. Early laws of the Massachusetts Bay Colony required an innkeeper to provide for a man, his horses, and his cattle.

The Hunt-Raymond-Bishop house is seen here. The Hunts lived here for several generations. Brothers Newell and Sewell Hunt sold the house to George J. Raymond in 1903. The owner of Raymond's Department Stores in Boston, Raymond was known for treating his employees fairly. In fact, employee Frank I. Dorr became president after Raymond's death in 1915. (Photograph by Donald D. Bishop.)

Twig Bridge was located on the Raymond farm at 80 Raymond Road. The pond was to be excavated by a local contractor in 1906. When Raymond asked the contractor how long it would take, the contractor replied that it would take 11 days. Raymond asked how many men he would need. The answer was three. Raymond replied, "Why don't you use 11 men and get it done in three days?" And so it was done.

John P. Bartlett, the son of the founder of Bartlett Greenhouses, poses in one of the family greenhouses, surrounded by geraniums. John was an engineer and developed many ways to increase production of what the Bartlett Greenhouses have become famous for: geraniums in all their resplendent colors and their greenery. The greenhouses are located at 578 Boston Post Road.

This was the home of one of America's greatest architects, Ralph Adams Cram, known for his American Gothic style. Cram is most famous for his design of St. John the Divine Church in New York City and many chapels in major universities, such as Princeton. He purchased this modest New England tavern/farmhouse in 1900 and turned it into the fine Federal-style home that still stands today at 427 Concord Road. He lived here year-round from 1930 on.

King Philip Farm was at the corner of Old Lancaster and Concord Roads, near 160 Concord Road. It was built in 1877 by the Hunt family. Patriarch Aaron Hunt was very well-to-do and had acquired a large estate before his death in 1877. The SHS has a collection of deeds for this property dating back to 1838. The parish house for Our Lady of Fatima Catholic Church now occupies this space.

Ellms family members sit in front of their house at 357 Boston Post Road. Asahel F. Ellms was a farmer, raising chickens in South Sudbury for decades. In 1890, he owned the house, the hen house, and the half-acre of land it was set on. This house still retains the Cape Cod style but no longer has a center chimney. It is now used as business offices and has a recessed entrance.

The Nahum Goodnow house is located at 163 Landham Road. It is a Queen Anne–style house built from 1884 to 1886. Nahum was the grandson of John Goodnow, who originally owned the property and whose estate sold it to Nahum after John's death. Nahum Goodnow lived from 1843 to 1897 and was a vegetable farmer. The house is still owned by Goodnow relatives.

The Grange Hall was formerly the Center Schoolhouse in 1849. Shortly after it was built, the building was lifted up and a first floor was added. It served all eight grades until it was condemned by the state for not having good air. It was sold at auction to the Grange in 1891. The Sudbury Grange is a fraternal order that continues to hold its meetings there today. This photograph was taken by Victor Neumeier during the American bicentennial in 1976, when it was the bicentennial headquarters.

This gristmill is being built for Henry Ford's Wayside Inn village complex. Ford wanted everything to look as picturesque as possible. He used this team of oxen to help move materials to the sites, but around back, the men were using a modern truck for the real work—a Ford, of course.

The Wayside Inn Gristmill is located at 131 Wayside Inn Road. Construction of the mill was started in 1927 on the orders of Henry Ford and completed in 1929. Ford wanted it to be built as an example of the use of waterpower and automation. John B. Campbell of Philadelphia designed the mill. The exterior is cut stone from Mount Nobscot and other local Ford land. It is still a working mill, grinding flour and cornmeal for the Wayside Inn.

The Wayside Inn Boys' School utilized all of the Wayside Inn Estate. The former Calvin Howe house at 150 Wayside Inn Road, which is now an empty lot, was the main school and a partial dormitory for the 75 students attending in 1943. Henry Ford believed in education and learning trades of a practical nature. The boys helped build the Martha Mary Chapel that is also on the grounds of the inn.

In 1923, when Henry Ford purchased the inn and surrounding land, he hired William W. Taylor to search out objects and buildings in New England that would be used in the New England village he was creating around the inn's 2,995 acres. This cider press is one of thousands of objects that were purchased. The apples were placed between the block, and the tray and the block's heavy weight pressed the juice into the barrel below.

The Wayside Inn has many intimate rooms. This was once the Ford Sitting Room and is now called the Inn Keeper's Room and is used for dining. In 1979, Robert Spaulding made one-inch-to-one-foot models of the inn, the gristmill, the chapel, and the Redstone Schoolhouse, and they were displayed in this room. The models were later given to the SHS. (Photograph by Victor Neumeier.)

The Redstone Schoolhouse—also called the Mary Lamb Schoolhouse—at 9 Dutton Road was originally located on the side of Redstone Hill in Sterling. The school had been torn down but the wood was recycled into a barn/garage. Henry Ford bought the barn, dismantled it, and brought it to Sudbury in 1926, where, after extensive research, it was reassembled as close to the original school as possible.

The Knight-Dutton Gristmill was on Dutton Road, where the Hop Brook goes under it at 181 Dutton Road. Joel and Samuel Knight built the mill in 1780 and operated it. A West India goods store was run by them on the nearby Dutton farm. Hattie Goodnow took this rare photograph and one other of the mill in 1899. The mill was powered by an interior turbine, thus it had no exterior wheel that could freeze in the winter. The mill was on the right side of the driveway, and only its foundation stones still exist.

An acre a day of hay could be cut by one man with a good, light European scythe. Mowing grass was a meditative experience—step and swing, swing and step, working one's way down the field, then looking over one's shoulder to view with pride the neat, straight line of mown grass, and breathing the aroma of freshly cut hay. (Photograph by Hattie Goodnow.)

Harvesting ice was a common occupation but it was quite arduous to cut, haul, and store the ice. Sudbury had a few independent ponds with spring-fed water that was not tied into the Hop Brook water system of ponds and streams. This photograph shows Blanchard's Pond on the Cavicchio farm. Their ice was for their own use, and they had an insulated icehouse to carry it through the summer.

The Dave Marshall house, built in 1900 at 354 Boston Post Road, is now the Sudbury Music Center. Marshall worked at the Hurlbut and Rogers machine shop behind the present Mill Village shopping district.

Hattie Goodnow was able to trip her camera lens and take self-portraits. Here, she poses with a bust of an Indian in the house, showing off her ability to compose a photograph well in 1903.

The town hall was dedicated on February 22, 1932. It was a larger replica of the old town house, which burned in 1930. The hall was built to be fireproof. The architect was Charles H. Way of Sudbury. Note the telephone and electric lines overhead that were buried in the center at great but worthwhile expense in the mid-1970s.

In 1947, Milton and Edna Swanson purchased the general store, which had been closed after running from 1930 to 1938 on the Henry Ford estate, and reopened it as the Wayside Country Store. Milton's father, Fred Swanson, worked in the store and became identified with it. He is seen above in front of the potbelly stove with Attic, the first of the Siberian huskies used to haul goods out of snow-bound warehouses buried in the woods.

The Parmenter-Garfield general store was originally located in the town center at what is now Grinnell Park. Future president James Garfield once taught school on the second floor. In 1929, the store was purchased by Henry Ford and moved to 1015 Boston Post Road in Marlborough by cutting it in half and hauling it with teams of oxen in the winter. It was reopened in 1930 as the general store, and students at the Wayside Inn Boys' School worked there. Christmas celebrations were held out front in December.

The general store was reopened in 1930 by Henry Ford as the first restored country store in America. One could shop there and buy a wide assortment of goods, as seen in the displays. Ford's wife, Clara, was behind the project. She especially wanted to show farmers how to display and merchandise their own fruits and vegetables in the stand to the left of the building. She also encouraged many colonial crafts on the second floor of the store, including weaving and spinning.

The penny candy counter at the Wayside Country Store was featured in 1955 as having over 90 types of candy for sale for a penny. The counter was at the back of the store. Lines of eager customers extended all the way out the door for 100 feet on Sundays; it took 10 clerks just to service this counter and pack Memory Bags, which sold for 25¢ in the striped candy bag that Leona Johnson lent Milton Swanson to reproduce and use.

Ye Olde Barbeque Inn was located at 410 Boston Post Road in what had been the Sudbury Inn. As a young man in the 1920s, late town historian Forrest Bradshaw was employed as a night watchman/night clerk. When they went out of business, Bradshaw was paid with the inn's china service for 50 in lieu of cash. The china is white with a maroon stripe and is trademarked Shennago China, New Castle, Pennsylvania.

The Lucy Brackett House—also known as the Tillie Smith House—is at 218 Old Sudbury Road. It was built in the Greek Revival style in 1850. Brackett was a teacher at Sudbury School. Before her death, she gave donations to all the churches in town. The First Parish named a room after her, which had a working fireplace and was used for small meetings, to remember her for her thankfulness.

The Gvensk Kaffe Stuga, a Swedish coffeehouse in South Sudbury, was located at 394 Boston Post Road. Very popular in its day, it attracted customers from 50 miles around. Founded in 1928, it was run by Paul Ecke and his family. As the sign says, it really was "a little bit of Sweden." Swedish families who had arrived as immigrants around 1900 had moved up to the middle class by the 1940s and enjoyed a touch of their homeland with good Swedish food.

Henry Ford had a portable planing and sawmill in use from 1927 to 1929 on the Wayside Inn grounds, where workmen were building what would become the Wayside Inn Gristmill. In the center background, the mill's granite walls are up, with a roof. The interior of the gristmill is mostly chestnut, but includes pine as well. Later, the planing and sawmill was moved to the Dutton Road salvage yard and then down to Hager Pond in Marlborough after the 1938 hurricane.

The Wolbach farm was comprised of 100 acres at 18 Wolbach Road. Dr. S. Burt Wolbach was the Shattuck professor of pathology at Harvard Medical School from 1922 to 1954, receiving many honors. The Wolbach family used it as a summer home until it was given to the Sudbury Valley Trustees (SVT) by his son John Wolbach. SVT, a nonprofit group that oversees and purchases land for preservation, took it over in 2004 and carefully restored the home, barn, and grounds.

A record ice storm hit Sudbury and the Boston Post Road in 1915. This photograph was taken looking east from the corner of Concord Road. The house on the left is 354 Boston Post Road, which is now the Sudbury Music Center, and the house on the right is No. 357. The storm hit when horse and carriages were gradually losing out to automobiles and trucks. Previously, the snow had been rolled for the use of sleighs, but now with automobiles, plowing was necessary and was almost impossible in an ice storm with the equipment available at the time.

The Wayside Inn had a major fire at 2:00 a.m. on December 22, 1955. The fire department did its best but the inn sustained massive damage. The fire started in the back, progressed to the west wing, and then moved forward to the old part of the structure. The firemen had to cut through 18 inches of ice to get to the water from the inn's Josephine Pond. By 2:45 a.m., 11 pieces of equipment from four neighboring towns were helping to put out the fire.

This is the South Sudbury railroad station, opposite what is now 28 Union Avenue. It is called Union Avenue because it is the union of two different railroads, which cross at the station. The east-west line was the B&M Central Massachusetts line and the north-south line was the Hartford, New Haven, Framingham, and Lowell branch of the B&M. The station was torn down in 1955, and a small waiting room was built nearby, which is now a livery service.

Bowker's Store was at the corner of Haynes and Pantry Roads. Some think it was the North Sudbury railroad station, but it was not; Everett W. Bowker and his wife tended store here for more than 40 years. It served the public as a general store, a gas station, and the North Sudbury Post Office. It closed sometime after 1961.

Ruth and Hank Greenblatt are dressed in their uniforms for the opening of their store, "Hello Deli."

The new truck "Little Lisa" ran into a train, resulting in this unique photograph at the intersection of the B&M railroad line at 394 Boston Post Road in 1955. George Halloran used to be the gatekeeper for the crossing, which was extremely dangerous. The railroad provided a little white shack for him to sit in with a heater, and when a train came, he would crank down the gates to stop traffic. This accident happened after he was laid off without a replacement.

Hall Realty hosts an open house in the 1960s. Their business was located in Enoch Kidder's building at 361 Boston Post Road, next to the present-day Mill Village. The employees were, from left to right, Bob Ayers, Jessie Hall, Earl Midgely, and Lorraine and Bill Hall. The Halls still live in Sudbury.

In 1902, the Thomas Elbridge Bent estate sale was of great interest to the townspeople. His house was located at 531 Concord Road. Bent, who was born in 1812, had inherited it from his father. Rachel H. Bent was the administrator of Bent's estate and sold the property. After 108 years, in 2010, basketball player Shaquille O'Neal leased part of the original property, located behind the house, while he played for the Boston Celtics.

DRAMA · SUPPER · CHARADES

AND

MUSICAL

ENTERTAINMENT

AT

TOWN HALL, SUDBURY,

FRIDAY EVE'G, MAR. 31, '93

SUDBURY GRANGE, NO. 121,

WILL PRESENT

NEVADA or the LOST MINE

A Drama in Three Acts, with the following Cast of Characters:

..., the Wanderer . . . . . Edward Brown	Jube, a Black Miner	Edgar W. Goodnow
'ermont, an Old Miner . . . . . George Thompson	Win Kye, a Chinaman	C. E. Haynes, Jr.
m Carew Young Miners . . . . Charles E. Ellms	Mother Murton	Emma F. Perry
...ndy Dick . . . . Harry W. Gilbert	Agnes Fairlee	Emily F. Willis
Silas Steele, Missionary of Health . . . E. W. Rice	Moselle, a Waif	Cora F. Whitney
Jerden, a Detective . . . . . Allen Sherman		

Musical Director, Miss Elinor M. Gerry.   Stage Manager, Mrs. A. W. Rice.

Supper at close of Drama. Then come Three Original Charades with prizes for first correct answer.

DON'T

forget the date.
forget the hour.
stay at home.
forget to come and bring someone with you.

Doors open at 7.15.   Curtain rises at 8, sharp.

No Reserved Seats!

ADULTS, 25 CTS. CHILDREN, under 12 10 CTS.

THE TRIBUN   EW PRESS.

In 1893, the town hall was the host site for this play put on by the member of the Grange. Sudbury was a farming community and the Grange was organized by farmers to be the voice of the farmers, cloaked in fraternal garb and ritual. Many of the people featured in these pages took part in this play, staying up until midnight and then rising with the roosters.

Visit us at
arcadiapublishing.com

www.ingramcontent.com/pod-product-compliance
Lightning Source LLC
Chambersburg PA
CBHW050559110426

42813CB00008B/2403